6 Keys to Kick-Start Your Dream

The Simple Guide to Unlocking the Greatness Within

Kelley Perry

Published by:

Kelley Perry
Waldorf, Maryland 20603

©2014 Kelley Perry All rights reserved. No part of this report may be reproduced or transmitted in any form or by any means, electronically or mechanically, including photocopying, recording, retrieval system, without prior written permission from the author, except for the inclusion of brief quotes in a review.

Editing by: Robin Devonish Scott- The Self Publishing Maven
Cover design by: Pro_Ebookcovers

Requests for permission to make copies of any part of this e-book can be made to Kelley Perry at kelley@coachkelleyperry.com

ISBN-13: 978-0991298044
ISBN-10: 0991298047
www.coachkelleyperry.com
Waldorf, Maryland
Printed in the United States

Dedication

This book is dedicated to my awesome husband, Ira, who has stood beside me and continued to encourage me to go for my dreams!

Thanks for being a great example and a wonderful friend and husband.

I love you with all my heart, forever and always.

Table of Contents

Introduction — vi

Key 1 Define Your Dream — 1

Key 2 Dig Deep for Your Why — 12

Key 3 Visualize Your Dream — 22

Key 4 Develop a Proper Mindset — 27

Key 5 Build Your Dream Team — 36

Key 6 Go for the Dream — 44

Introduction

If you are reading this book, I'm sure you have a dream, a desire, and most likely many ideas, such as starting a business, going back to school, changing careers, moving to a new city, losing weight, changing your outlook on life, or many other things you may want to do; but are unsure how to make them happen.

Perhaps you are one who has stepped out and gone after your dreams or pursued your ideas, but then things didn't happen the way you visualized. So you put it down and now are wondering if you should go for it again. Or maybe you just have the idea and you have done nothing about it because you have allowed fear to hold you back. I say, it doesn't matter which one you are. Allow me to encourage you to get off the couch of comfort, let go of those negative feelings caused by a lack of accomplishment, and go after your dreams with passion.

The feeling of having a dream but not knowing what to do can be very frustrating; believe me, I know how it feels. I have been on many sides of the dilemma: Having a dream and not doing anything with it; stopping a dream because I tried to pursue it in the past and only got discouraged and hurt; talking myself out of a dream, only to go back to dreaming again.

I am so excited you are reading this book. I have written it with the following goals:

1. To share the "Keys" of kick-starting your dream.
2. To set you on course to going ahead and living your dreams.

So congratulations! You have started the journey by picking up the right book.

Key 1

Define Your Dream

"The dream is not what you see in sleep, dream is what does not let you sleep!"
—Dr. Abdul Kalam

Let's start by defining exactly what a dream is. According to the *Merriam-Webster Dictionary*, the first definition of "dream" is: "a series of thoughts, images, or emotions occurring during sleep." Our dreams are not something we only have when we sleep, but those images and thoughts birth something on the inside that affects not only our sleeping habits but also begins to control parts of our life. I want to share that my dreams won't let me sleep because they long to be a part of my reality. I often make the comment: "Keep dreaming, and when you wake up go do what you saw in your dreams." I have learned that our dreams don't want to be trapped in our sleep time; they want to become our reality, and they are so real you have to ask: "Is this real or am I dreaming?

Your dreams provide hope, expectation for the future, and a visual road map for where you desire to go. Your dreams show you some of the details of where you're going, but not how you'll get there. This is the part that many people have trouble with. The dream doesn't show you everything because you have the responsibility to get on the path of making that dream become your life's reality. Also, it's not just about getting to the end of the dream; it's about the journey through and to the dream. The passage not only prepares you, but it develops you so that when you reach the goal of your dream, you have grown and matured, and you can appreciate what it took to get there. The journey will also test your belief and the tenacity you possess to make the dream become reality. If you don't believe your dreams will come true, they won't. You have to have faith and then apply the proper corresponding actions, which will lead you to the results you desire.

Is this the time to get up and make your dream happen? Are you ready for change? Are you tired of not living life to the fullest? Don't you want something different for your life? I hope you yelled a loud "YES" to those questions and are now asking: "What do I do now?" A few years ago, I was screaming "YES" and searching to find a way to do something different. My biggest question was: "How can I get these ideas and dreams from inside my head and put them in action outside?" If that is what you are saying to yourself, you definitely have the right book before you, and it is your time to step out and into your passion, purpose, and dreams.

Let's move toward the next step by taking a few moments to write down your dream. But, before you do this, please think about these questions:

1. What is it you "Love" doing and are "Willing" to do without pay?
2. What is the "Problem" you see for which without much effort you have the answer or are able to fix?
3. As a child, what did you pretend to be? What did you daydream about?

Now, write down your answers to these questions, and be confident in your responses. Don't second-guess yourself.

Even if you think it is silly, just write down what comes to mind without crossing anything out. Use as many details as possible, and ask yourself questions like:

    A. What do I see myself doing?

    B. Who am I doing it for?

    C. Who will be impacted the most?

    D. While doing it, does it include traveling, writing, singing, etc.?

    E. What resources do I need to make it happen?

    F. Where will it take place?

    G. Can I do it by myself, or will I need help?

    H. Once I pursue it, how will it make me feel?

These are just a few questions to get you started. This exercise may take one day or two, but it is very necessary to assist you in "Defining Your Dream."

Below is your area to start answering the questions provided and describe your dream. If you have more than one dream, start with the one that comes to mind first.

Dream Work: Below, please write out your dream in detail, and don't concern yourself with the "How."

I'm so excited that you put in the time to write out your dream. I believe this is a very important key in order for you to pursue that dream. Look at this as a contract with yourself and your dream that gives you the vision to see where you're going.

You can do this. Don't try to figure everything out right now. If you continue to read this book, I am confident it will all come together for you.

Key 2

Dig Deep for Your Why

*"You see things; and you say Why?
But I dream things that never were;
and I say Why not?"*
—George Bernard Shaw

Now that you have finished writing down your dream, let's move on and dig deep.

The next key to achieving your dream is to understand and know your "WHY." Yes, the why is the most important factor, because if you don't know the reason why you want to pursue your dream, what will keep you going when all looks bleak? Your "WHY" is what will keep you from staying discouraged, throwing in the towel, and calling it quits. I have learned that when your why is BIG and DEEP enough, you will undoubtedly reach your goals. You see clearer on your journey despite the obstacles, setbacks, and problems that WILL come up. Believe me, on those difficult days you will reflect on your why, and that is what will keep you going.

So, you may be asking: "What do I mean when I say your WHY?" Allow me to share one of my dreams. Several years ago, I woke up with this idea for a teen girls program. I wrote the idea down and began to ponder: "How could I make this happen?" I had a really good friend who knew a little more than me about putting programs together. After discussing it with my friend, we came up with a name, filed our incorporation paperwork, wrote out our vision, and developed our programs—and BAM! We were in business. I found a place to hold our classes and workshops, and we began to purchase equipment and decorate the center. Six months later, however, things were not going the way I had envisioned. My partner went back to work, and I was left sitting in a fully equipped room ready to help teenage girls, but I had very few teenage girls coming in. Three months after that, I was packing up, and the dream was over. Why? Because I had no why! I didn't take the time to sit down and determine why I wanted that dream to come true.

Even though the program would serve a great purpose, it didn't have a greater purpose within me. I had nothing deep within me that moved me to keep going even though I didn't see the clients or the money coming in. So guess what? I quit. When I ran into some resistance, I allowed it to push me out. If I would have taken the time to determine why this was so important to me, I could have reflected during those hard times on what would have inspired me to keep going.

Now, here is an example of someone with a why: One of my clients wanted to buy a house. Yes, her dream was to own her own home. The reason she wanted to own her own home was because as a child her mom used to move around a lot. In one year, they moved six times and she was never able to make any childhood friends or have a place she could call home. At the point of our conversation, she herself was a mother of three and didn't want her children to grow up like that. She wanted to give her children a home. That was her why: "Giving her children a place they could call home."

Now every time she faced an obstacle or an adverse situation, she would reflect on that why. So, when Macy's, Nordstrom's, or DSW had a sale on shoes, and when her girlfriends wanted to go on shopping trips, she forfeited because she was working on something.

She would see the end and the reason she wanted to get there. This helped her to keep her money in the bank and move her closer to her dream becoming reality for herself and her children. Because she stayed true to her why, it wasn't long before she had her dream home. It was her "WHY" that motivated her to save her money and resist the many temptations. So, I ask you: "How bad do you want it?" You have to want it really, really bad. It has to be DEEP within and mean so much to you that it would hold your feet to the path of victorious reality. Now, take some time to think about your why—and yes, we are going to write it down.

Take some time to really search within and find out "WHY" you want to pursue your DREAMS! Think to yourself:

    A. What will happen if I don't go after the dream?

    B. Will I be OK if the dream remains a dream?

    C. Who will miss out on the impact of my dream?

After spending some time thinking, and I mean really digging deep, go ahead and begin writing your big "WHY"!

Dream Work: Find a place where you can focus, and think about why you want to pursue your dreams. Use the space provided here to "Dig Deep for Your Why."

I'm so proud of you for taking the time to dig deep and discover your why. Sometimes during this process, you may cry because you realize how important it is to go for your dreams. You have just created your anchor that will hold you steady as you go for your dream.

Key 3

Visualize Your Dream

"Dream and give yourself permission to envision a You that you choose to be."
—Joy Page

Let's recap briefly. You know where you're going and why. Now is the time to begin the journey. You've just written a dream roadmap. Now is the time to add visualization. Through visualization, we create mental images of our desired results, which is important to moving the dream into reality.

When you see yourself in your dream, it begins to build the inward confidence that you can and will accomplish your dreams. Jerry West, the NBA logo, had a reputation for hitting buzzer beaters. West shared the reason he had so much success with that shot; he had hit those shots repeatedly in his mind.

West and many other athletes, artists, CEOs, and at-home moms have recognized the power of visualization. Whenever I have taken the time to create pictures in my mind and spend time thinking of them, I begin to see my confidence grow and my mindset move to "Yes, I will obtain my dreams!"

You can also create a vision/dream board. You do this by using poster boards and old magazines. This exercise will help build another point of reflection to help with visualization. When going through the magazines, you want to choose pictures and words that speak to you and cause something inside you to say, "*Yes*, that represents the images and ideas for my dream."

I have placed examples of my vision/dream board in the back of this book to give you an idea of what one looks like. Don't feel as if you have to make yours look exactly like mine. I have done this exercise more than once with my children, and they always get upset because they think mine looks better than theirs do. I tell them that my map speaks to me as your map should speak to you. This exercise is not to give a grade, but to give you a picture of the dream fulfilled. I believe you are serious about reaching your goals and dreams, so go ahead and begin to visualize your results and see yourself living in your dreams.

Dream Work: Take some time to create a dream/vision board. Decide, also, to spend time daily to visualize living in your dreams. Write how the dream/vision board moves you when you look at it and how this exercise is building your confidence to reach your dream.

I'm so excited about the progress you are making on your dream. When you complete your "Dream Map," take a picture of it and send it to Kelley@coachkelleyperry.com. I would love to see what your map looks like! Make it a habit to look at your dream map often. This will help you to keep the vision fresh and bring further clarity to where you're going.

Key 4

Develop a Proper Mindset

"A dream doesn't become reality through magic; it takes sweat, determination and hard work." —Colin Powell

You are well on your way to pursuing your DREAM! You have discovered the foundational elements, and now it's time to make sure that your mind is properly focused to nurture, develop, and sustain your dream.

A few years ago the National Science Foundation discovered that our brains could produce over 50,000 thoughts a day. Wow, 50,000 thoughts that consist of worries, guilt, things we didn't do, things we could've done, hurts, mistakes, thoughts about the future, and plenty of thoughts about the past. Of all those thoughts that we're having, most of them will not help sustain the dream unless we begin to exchange those negative, nonproductive thoughts with more positive, productive thoughts that will help nurture, develop, and fulfill the dream to its highest potential.

Now, you may be asking: "How can I do that?" The answer is this: Become mindful of your thoughts. We have the power to decide whether we dwell on a thought or get rid of it. I challenge you to focus on your thoughts for a day—pick a day to do this—be aware of all the thoughts that go through your mind, and write them down. At the end of the day look them over, and see what your thoughts are telling you. Are we in control of the thoughts that run through our minds? Our thoughts determine whether we will experience a happy or gloomy or doomed life.

Now that you have seen for yourself how your thoughts can be everywhere but where you want them, what will you do now?

Here are a few suggestions to help you:

1) Recognize those moments of negative thoughts; stop and replace them with more positive, productive thoughts.

2) Find optimistic, authentic, and happy people to connect with and take notice of the things they say and how they view their lives.

3) Do your best to limit the amount of negatives in your life.

4) Do things that make you happy. Your dream, of course, should be one of them.

5) Find a place to volunteer. When you help others, it causes you to feel grateful;

it gives you a more encouraging view of life.

6) Read or listen to books about the life journey of others. Pay close attention to how they were able to follow their dreams and reach their goals.

Make it a priority to possess a mind that is clutter-free and productive so that you can grow and develop your mind properly. There is a saying, "As a man thinks so is he," which means: "What you decide to dwell on the most is what you will experience or see the most." Do you see how important it is to have a successful mindset in order to live your dream?

A successful mindset is not just thinking positively and waiting for things to happen. With a successful mindset, you will move into action and make things happen. I firmly believe that your mindset is a very important key to pursuing your goals, dreams, and passions. If you are going to win, you will win it in your mind first.

Dream Work: How committed are you to developing and maintaining a "Proper Mindset"? Below, list some of the things you will do to develop and maintain that proper mindset.

I am so excited you have chosen to take action now to work on your mindset so that your dreams will have the best opportunity to grow.

Key 5

Build Your Dream Team

Great things in business are never done by one person; they're done by a team of people.— Steve Jobs

You are making great progress. Now it's time to build a team. I believe that everyone needs a "Dream Team." Every great movie has a star and a supporting cast. Every great sports player has a team to help him or her make the big plays. Michael Jordan was a great basketball player, but if he didn't have a team, someone to guard the other players, someone to pass him the ball so he could score, he wouldn't be known as one of the best ever. It took a team to do that, a "Dream Team."

Now understand that I'm not necessarily talking about the people who will help you create or build a company. I'm talking about a team of people that will push, encourage, and support you on your journey. Your team may include people who work with you directly or indirectly.

I remember when I first started building my coaching business. I had a friend who would send me encouraging tweets. When we met in person, my friend was always excited about my progress and encouraged me to keep going. The support through tweets, words of encouragement, and genuine excitement helped to push me to my success. She became a part of my dream team, and didn't even know it.

As you build your dream team, know that it may not include family or friends, because they may not understand why you would want to leave your "good" job and start your own business, or why you would want to make life changes now. So, don't be upset if you ask them for their support and they let you down. Look to those who may or may not understand what you are doing, but who are willing to commit to supporting you.

I remember an occasion when I decided to lose 20 pounds before going to a conference; I asked three people I knew to hold me accountable. Out of the three, two of them held my feet to the fire. If they saw me eating something they knew I was not supposed to be eating, they checked me. They would call and check in on me; they would ask me how the workouts were going; and they celebrated with me as I met certain milestones. Their support was exactly what I needed to keep me on the path to my dream. And guess what, I lost the weight!

As you think about the different people you want to be part of your team, I encourage you to choose a variety. Your "Dream Team" doesn't need to be in your own field of business or doing anything like what you are doing. Remember, they will be the people you can bounce ideas off; they will be the people who give you their opinion on certain things. Most of all, they will be people who will keep you accountable, give you support, share a kind word of encouragement, or kick you in the rear to keep you going for your dream. Your "Team" will cheer you toward your DREAM!

Dream Work: List the names of some people you believe would be great to have on your Dream Team. Then call them up and see if they would be willing to support you on your journey.

_____

_____

_____

_____

_____

_____

_____

_____

_____

_____

_____

Every dream has a supporting cast! Go ahead and put your Dream Team together so they can assist you in making your imaginings come true.

Key 6

Go for the Dream

"Every great dream begins with a dreamer. Always remember, you have within you the strength, the **patience**, *and the passion to reach for the stars to change the world."*
—Harriet Tubman

Look at how far you have come! Are you excited about the progress you've made? I am! Let's do one more recap of what you've accomplished:

First: You "Defined" your dream by stating what you wanted to do and what doing it would mean to you by writing down your thoughts in detail.

Second: You took a step further to "Dig Deep" to discover your why. By doing this, it enabled you to understand how the "Why" will sustain you in the difficult times.

Third: You "Visualized" your dream by creating a book or board filled with images and words that were special to you only.

Fourth: You realized how the "Proper Mindset" can be hard to maintain over your thoughts since on average we have over 50,000 thoughts per day. You learned the importance of connecting with optimistic people and controlling thoughts that keep you from being positive and productive.

Fifth: You made a list of your "Team," individuals who will cheer you on to your "Dream." These people will cheer you on, hold you accountable, and be in your corner when you need them.

Now it is time to Go For It! You have read through this entire book; and you have done the exercises. Now it is time to do it, to accomplish your dream.

It takes courage to have a dream and to step out and do what's necessary for that dream to become a reality. Many dream but are unwilling to do the work.

They start the work but give up when things get hard. But not you!

You have continued the journey, and there is a reward for those of you willing to hang in there and do the work. The reward is the opportunity to live your DREAM!

The lessons you learn, the changes you make, and the growth that takes place is what makes the dream. Without all of that, you would not see or experience it. Take the time to enjoy every part of the ride! Journal about it; take pictures; laugh, cry, learn, and live life to the fullest!

Before I started going for my dreams, I lived an unfulfilled life; my life was without purpose. On the inside, I wanted something more; but outside there was nothing to reassure me that I could have it. When I finally made up my mind to pursue my dream of building a business, I had to overcome my limiting thoughts, rebuild my mindset, step out of my comfort zone, and be willing to fail forward.

I remember one time when I registered to attend a networking event out of my area. I was going to a new place where I wouldn't know anyone. On my way to the event, I got lost in an area where there was no cell phone coverage. I pulled over to the side of the road and felt like crying. Then, I began to remind myself why I was there on the side of the road. It was not because I was lost; I was there because I wanted to go for my dream. I began to give myself a pep talk and decided to drive until I could get coverage.

When I finally arrived at the event, my fear tried to hinder me from going in. However, I decided that I no longer wanted to "merely" exist. I wanted my life to mean something. I wanted to go for my DREAM! I literally jumped out of the car and moved as fast as I could to the door. Because I kept moving forward, my life has not been the same since.

I hope this book reminds you that your dream can become your reality and encourages you to join me in going for your dream.

Dream Work: Now is the time to write down what you are "Going For." What are you willing to commit to do this week to keep your dream moving? Who do you need to talk to? Where do you need to go? What book do you need to read? What conference, workshop, or networking event should you attend?

Date:_____

1 Goal for Today
_____
_____

#2 Goal for Today
_____
_____

#3 Goal for Today
_____
_____

Accomplishments
1.
2.
3.
4.
5.

Challenges
1.
2.
3.
4.
5.

Date:_____

1 Goal for Today
_____
_____

#2 Goal for Today
_____
_____

#3 Goal for Today
_____
_____

Accomplishments
1.
2.
3.
4.
5.

Challenges
1.
2.
3.
4.
5.

Write your thoughts about the day. Further assess your accomplishments and challenges.

My personal affirmation for today is:

Use the chart daily. Make it a habit that you are doing something every day to make your dreams a reality.

About the Author

Kelley Perry is a business start-up consultant, dream coach, and speaker.

She enjoys helping those who suffer from what she calls "scatterbrainism." They have so many great ideas, but they are unsure what to do first, so they usually end up doing nothing. She helps you organize your thoughts, goals, and dreams so you can experience profitability in your life and business.

Kelley firmly believes that everyone has a divine purpose. With guidance, direction, and a plan, everyone can fulfill his or her God-given purpose.

Kelley served nine years in the United States Army working in communications and logistics. Kelley obtained a bachelor's in business administration with a concentration in management. She is married to her best friend and business partner, Ira, and they have five beautiful daughters. www.coachkelleyperry.com

One of my "Dream Maps"

www.ingramcontent.com/pod-product-compliance
Lightning Source LLC
Chambersburg PA
CBHW071638040426
42452CB00009B/1689